pink Scallop

silver birch

This notebook has been put together for you to take out on all your expeditions into the great outdoors – whether it's your back garden, the local park, the woods, the beach or the open countryside. We've packed it with ideas and identification charts to help you explore in the wild. Learn how to identify birds, go pond dipping or build a shelter. We've left lots of space for you to fill with drawings and stories of your adventures, as well as places for you to log and record your discoveries. Just pop *The Adventurer's Notebook* in your backpack and head off.

This notebook belongs to

. . . .

ADVENTURER'S ESSENTIALS

Every adventurer needs to check supplies before setting out. Here is an essential list plus some suggestions for extra supplies if you are going further afield. Remember to always tell someone where you are going and when you expect to be back.

- Water
- Snacks
- First aid kit with plasters and bite and sting cream or spray
- Compass
- Adventurer's Notebook
- Pencil
- A whistle – in case someone gets lost
- Pocket knife
- Rucksack or bag

Extra Supplies

- Plastic bags or small boxes for storing finds
- Camera
- Fishing line and hook
- Nets or old sieves for pond dipping
- Garden scissors
- String
- Magnifying glass
- Torch
- Bug box
- Wellington boots
- A rug or something to sit on
- Bag to take any rubbish away

Adventurer's Snack

This is an easy-to-make high-energy snack (based on a New Zealand recipe), to take on expeditions. Mix together raisins, sultanas, nuts, chocolate (Smarties or chocolate buttons are good), dried fruits, seeds and toasted oats in any combination you like.

MY LIST

WILDLIFE WATCHING

Take some time out and sit completely still for a few moments to listen and watch for wildlife. Animals are very sensitive to noise and can be hard to spot. What is easier to find are the clues they leave behind – where they have been, what they have been eating and what they have been up to. Evidence is all around you if you know what to look for. When you are out and about gather what you can from the list below to help you identify the animals around you.

what to look for
- feathers
- chewed pine cones
- nuts or seeds
- broken eggshells
- low tunnels in the bushes that cut across the footpath
- tracks in the mud
- dung
- bones and skulls

When you find something
- draw a sketch
- take a photograph
- write a description of what it looks like and how it behaves
- describe any distinct sounds or smells you notice

Animal tracks

☐ Badger   ☐ Muntjac Deer   ☐ Fox

ANIMALS I HAVE SEEN

❏ Badger

❏ Bat

❏ Deer

❏ Fox

❏ Frog

❏ Hedgehog

❏ Horse

❏ Mouse

❏ Rabbit

❏ Squirrel

❏ Toad

❏ Water Shrew

ANIMALS I HAVE SEEN

Name of animal   Where and when

Description

Draw a picture

ANIMALS I HAVE SEEN

Name of animal

Where and when

Description

Draw a picture

draw a picture of what you have seen

BIRD WATCHING

Bird watching can be great fun and is easy to do. You can start in your back garden or local park. What birds you see will depend on the time of year and where you are. Different birds like to live in different kinds of places, by water, in woods and in gardens. It is worth finding out which species are most common around your area.

Start by borrowing a pair of binoculars to get a closer look. Very quickly you will learn to identify particular birds by the colours of their feathers, their size, their beaks and their bird song. To help you recognise them look at the clues below.

If you are not sure what species a bird is, ask yourself the following questions and write down the answers in this notebook so you can look them up when you are at home. Draw a picture and label it to remind yourself of particular characteristics.

How to identify birds

- What size is the bird? Is it bigger/smaller than a robin (or choose a bird you know well)
- What colour are its feathers? What colours are where?
- What shape is its beak? What colour is it?
- How long are its legs? What colour are they?
- What kind of feet does it have? Are they webbed?
- What kind of tail does it have? Long or short?
- Describe the sounds it makes.
- Make a note of exactly where you saw the bird, the time of day, season and date.

❏ Swan

WATER BIRDS I HAVE SEEN

❑ Avocet

❑ Black-headed Gull

❑ Coot

❑ Cormorant

❑ Curlew

❑ Duck

❑ Great Crested Grebe

❑ Heron

❑ Little Egret

❑ Marsh Harrier

❑ Oystercatcher

❑ Redshank

BIRDS I HAVE SEEN

Name of bird

Where and when

Description

Draw a picture

BIRDS I HAVE SEEN

Name of bird   Where and when

Description

Draw a picture

WOOD AND GARDEN BIRDS I HAVE SEEN

❑ Barn Owl

❑ Blue Tit

❑ Great Spotted
Woodpecker

❑ Jay

❑ Linnet

❑ Pigeon

❑ Pheasant

❑ Red Kite

❑ Robin

❑ Rook

❑ Starling

❑ Swift

BIRDS I HAVE SEEN

Name of bird   Where and when

Description

Draw a picture

BIRDS I HAVE SEEN

Name of bird

Where and when

Description

Draw a picture

INSECTS I HAVE SEEN

☐ Blue Butterfly

☐ Damselfly

☐ Dragonfly

☐ Dungbeetle

☐ Honey Bee

☐ Ladybird

☐ Pale Clouded Yellow Butterfly

☐ Pond Skater

☐ Red Admiral Butterfly

Go on a bug hunt

See how many different kinds of bugs you can find. A good place to search is under rocks, logs and leaves. Creepy crawlies like to live in dark damp places. They like munching on rotting vegetation. When you find one count how many legs it has got, see what colour it is and whether it has any spots. Always remember to cover the bugs back up afterwards.

INSECTS I HAVE SEEN

Name of insect   Where and when

Description

Draw a picture

INSECTS I HAVE SEEN

Name of insect   Where and when

Description

Draw a picture

TREES I HAVE SEEN

You can identify leaves by their shape. Here are some common leaf types but see if you can find and identify any others. Notice the texture and any unusual characteristics other than shape. You can draw or make a leaf rubbing by placing a piece of paper over your leaf and rubbing with a crayon.

❑ Ash

❑ English Oak

❑ Hazel

❑ Horse Chestnut

❑ Lime

❑ London Plane

❑ Turkey Oak

❑ Silver Birch

❑ Sycamore

do a leaf rubbing

stick in some leaves you have found

WILD FLOWERS I HAVE SEEN

Find flowers in the hedgerows, meadows and fields. Spring and summer are the best times of year to go flower hunting. See how many varieties of different coloured flowers you can find. Sketch the flowers you have seen. To help identify them, pay special attention to the number and shape of the leaves, the number and colour of the petals and where and when you found them. Pick up fallen petals and press them between the pages of this book. Make your own flower fairy pictures and rhymes.

❑ Bramble   ❑ Cowslip   ❑ Daisy

❑ Dandelion   ❑ Dog Rose   ❑ Gorse

❑ Hawthorn, May   ❑ Nettle   ❑ Poppy

WILD FLOWERS I HAVE SEEN

Name of flower

Where and when

Description

Draw a picture

WILD FLOWERS I HAVE SEEN

Name of flower   Where and when

Description

Draw a picture

AT THE BEACH

Beach combing

Explore the beach looking for whelks eggs, mermaid's purse, crabs, razor shells, oyster shells, cockle shells, mussels, starfish, sea urchin, seaweed, bird feathers, scallop shells, jellyfish (don't touch), cuttlefish bones and driftwood. Make a note of what you have found in this notebook.

crabbing

All you need to go crabbing is a fishing line, a weight to hang on the line, some bacon (or similar) as bait, and a bucket of water to put the crabs in. Simply unravel a long stretch of line and tie your weight to the end of it.

A hagstone (a stone with a hole in it) is perfect for the job. Tie the bait to the line and then dangle the whole thing into the sea at the end of a quay, jetty or off a harbour wall. Pull the line up every now and then and see what you've got.

Sometimes you will have several crabs hanging from the line, or maybe just one big one. Haul it in and put your catch in the bucket of water. When you think you have enough crabs for a race, take the bucket up the beach and set them free. See how quickly they race back to the water. Give them names and allocate teams for added sport.

Rock pooling

Look in rock pools and see what the tide has left behind. Take a net and a bucket to store your trawl so that you can study them up close. You might find sea creatures such as starfish, limpets, sea urchins, winkles, shrimps and hermit crabs. Don't forget to put everything back afterwards.

AT THE BEACH

Stone skimming

You can do this at the seaside or on a river or lake. To spin a winning stone you will need: a flat stone, a low throw and a spin on the stone.

- Choose your stone carefully. Look for a round, flat stone that will fit nicely in the crook between your thumb and forefinger. Hold the stone in this crook, with your finger and thumb curling around the narrow edge.
- Face the water, making sure there is no one in front of you. Make sure there is no one behind you, either, in case you throw backwards by accident.
- Turn your body sideways to the water and bend your legs, pulling your arm back. Release the stone low above the surface, allowing the flat edge to skim the water.
- As you throw the stone pull your index finger back, imparting a spin to the stone to make it bounce across the water.

Something to do, something to make . . .

- Take an old bottle, a piece of paper and a pen to write a message. Seal it tight and throw it ceremoniously out to sea.
- When the tide is out, dig in the mudflats: discover ragworms, molluscs and mud beetles.
- Build a sandcastle.
- Make a sand picture using all of the things you have found.
- String hagstones together to make mobiles.
- Thread shells to make seaside jewellery.
- Find large pebbles and paint them. You can paint faces, turn them into flowers, animals or even monsters.
- Gather driftwood and make a sculpture.

SEASHELLS I HAVE SEEN

❑ Blue Mussel

❑ Common Edible Cockle

❑ Common Limpet

❑ Common Piddock

❑ Common Whelk

❑ Grooved Razor Clam

❑ Mermaid's Purse

❑ Noah's Ark

❑ Pink Scallop

❑ Striped Venus

❑ Weathervane Scallop

❑ Winkle

BY THE WATER

Pond dipping

Ponds are teeming with water creatures such as skaters, mayflies, dragonflies and damselflies on top of the water, and fish, frogs, tadpoles and water snails below the surface. To take a closer look prepare to get flat on your tummy. Take a jam jar and fill it with pond water. Check to see what you have already caught. Then dip a net or sieve in the pond and slowly pass it through the water. Empty your catch into the jar and, when the contents settle, see what you have caught. Identify it and record what you have found in this notebook. Carefully empty the jar back into the pond afterwards.

Frog spawn and tadpoles
The jelly of frog spawn contains hundreds of eggs, preparing to hatch into tadpoles. Over several weeks, limbs are formed, the tail shrinks and a frog is created. These frogs will one day try to come back to the same pond to lay their own eggs. Toad spawn looks very different and is laid in long ribbons, not in round clusters.

Dragonflies and damselflies
These live underwater for much of their lives and it is probably the larger dragonfly nymph that you will find when pond dipping. The hatched grub crawls to the surface. As the skin dries and hardens, it splits and releases the dragonfly to the air, coming back to the pond for drinking or to lay eggs.

Pond skater
The surface tension of the water is enough to keep these tiny creatures skimming along the top of the pond, sharing the weight load across each of its skinny, long legs.

Diving beetles
These beetles trap bubbles of air to keep them alive underwater. They move very quickly and are exciting to watch.

POND LIFE I HAVE SEEN

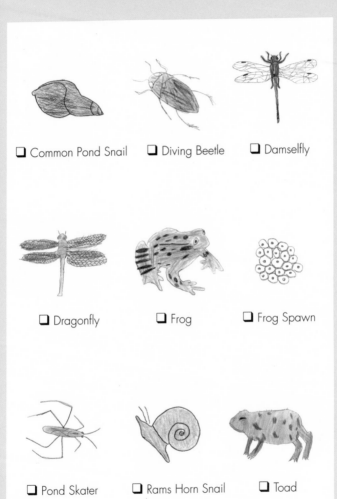

❑ Common Pond Snail   ❑ Diving Beetle   ❑ Damselfly

❑ Dragonfly   ❑ Frog   ❑ Frog Spawn

❑ Pond Skater   ❑ Rams Horn Snail   ❑ Toad

BY THE WATER

Make a paper boat

- Get a thick piece of A4 paper and some crayons.
- Lay the piece of paper out on a flat surface. Fold it in half vertically into a smaller rectangle.
- Fold down each corner on the creased edge into the centre line to form the sail shape.
- Fold one piece of the slim rectangular band up along the bottom of the triangle to form the side of the boat. Turn over and do the same on the other side.
- Colour in your boat, give it a name and sail number.
- From the bottom gently pull apart the sides of your boat. It is now ready to sail.

Why not make a fleet of boats and have a race . . .

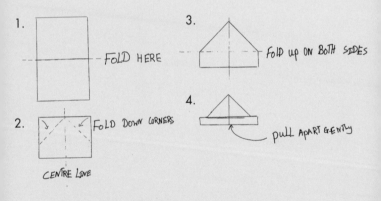

1.

— FOLD HERE

3.

— FOLD UP ON BOTH SIDES

2.

FOLD DOWN CORNERS

CENTRE LINE

4.

PULL APART GENTLY

OUT IN THE WILD

Shelter building

- Look around the woods and find three long, strong sticks or branches. One should be forked to act as a crook. The other two should be long enough to mark out the frame of your shelter.
- Lie on the ground to measure the size you need the shelter to be.
- Dig a small hole and plant your forked stick upright in it.
- Lean the other two sticks into the fork. The gap between them will be your entrance.
- Work your way around the shelter, filling the sides with straight sticks, leaning them against the two main branches. As they become more densely filled, find twigs with little branches off them to lay on top. These will serve to trap the top layer of leaves.
- When you think the shelter is ready, coat from top to bottom with dry leaves, several inches deep. Try not to gather soil with the leaves as this will just fall through the gaps on to you.
- Climb inside your shelter. This should be warm and dry and protect you from light rain.

Have a woodlouse race

These completely harmless creatures can be found under fallen branches, logs and old piles of rotting leaves, hiding from the daylight. Trap them carefully in matchboxes, giving them names if you like (Schumacher, Speedy, Hamilton). Create three race courses by clearing three areas in the earth, all of similar shape and size. Gently tip the racing woodlice into the centre of each area, still trapped under the matchbox. On the count of three (or ready, steady, go), lift the lid and see which creature gets to the edge first.

OUT IN THE WILD

Foraging for food

This is fun to do and anyone can do it. The hedges are full of things to eat. In the spring look out for: stinging nettles, elderflower and dandelions. In early summer, wild strawberries and wild garlic and in autumn, blackberries, rosehips and sweet chestnuts. Take some gloves and scissors with you. Think about where you are picking. Don't pick within dog peeing reach and always check with an adult before popping anything in your mouth.

Nettle soup recipe

INGREDIENTS

50g/2oz butter • 1 onion • 2 medium potatoes • 500ml/1 pint vegetable stock • 3 big handfuls of young stinging nettle leaves, gathered from the top of the plants • 200ml/$^1/_3$ pint single cream • salt and pepper

- Melt the butter in a pan.
- Finely chop the onion and cook until clear.
- Add the peeled and cubed potatoes and stir for a few minutes to glaze them with the butter.
- Add the vegetable stock and simmer for about ten minutes.
- Add the chopped-up nettles and stew for a few minutes until they have wilted.
- Add the cream and some salt and pepper to taste.

Nettle facts

- Did you know that nettles are full of vitamins A and C?
- Always pick the young leaves at the top of the plant as they will be more tender than those at the bottom.
- Don't eat raw nettles: cooking them neutralises the stinging agent in the plant.
- You can cook and eat nettles just like spinach.
- Green leaves taste much more bitter to children than adults. This may be evolutionary: the bitter taste acts as a deterrent to children and prevents them from eating things that might be poisonous.

OUT IN THE WILD

Scavenger hunting

Make a collection of things that you find in the wild. Gather whatever you can find. Here are some suggestions of the sorts of things that you might discover. Some of them you can pick up and take with you, others can be seen and recorded in this notebook.

GATHER	IDENTIFY
A round stone	An animal track
A feather	A bird's footprint
A seed	An animal burrow
A thorn	A bird's nest
A bone	Wild flowers
A piece of eggshell	Mushrooms and toadstools
A pine cone	A birdsong
A dandelion clock	A wild animal
Nuts and berries	Animal droppings

Devise a wild treasure hunt of your own ...

Something sticky	Something old
Something shiny	Something hollow
Something sharp	Something bitten
Something furry	Something rough
Something hairy	Something bright
Something brittle	Something smooth
Something bendy	Something spiked
Something round	Something forked

Ambushing

Smear your face with mud and earth, stick some leaves in your hair to camouflage yourself. Run ahead of the gang and see how well you can hide behind or up a tree, or under a bush. Use fallen leaves and branches to make yourself completely hidden. Stay still and silent. Jump out with a wild cry just at the moment the rest of the group passes by.

OUT IN THE WILD

Tracking and trail finding

Have some fun with a tracking expedition. Send a party of native trackers ahead of the main group to leave a trail of clues for them to follow.

Use simple arrows made of sticks or stones on the pathways to show the way. Mark paths with a cross if they are not the right way. Tie branches and leaves together to block a turning. Drop trails of pebbles, like Hansel and Gretel.

Decide which symbols you are going to use before you set off. Create your own secret set of symbols and signs if you wish.

THIS WAY ARROW

THIS WAY POINTER

TURN RIGHT

DO NOT GO THIS WAY

DO NOT GO THIS WAY STONES

THE RIGHT WAY STONES

GONE HOME

GONE HOME

OUT IN THE WILD

Something to do, something to make . . .

A quill pen
- Find a large bird feather.
- Cut the pointed end and shape into a nib.
- Dip it in some ink and give your signature a flourish.

A bow and arrow
- Cut a length of hazel or young, flexible wood, about three quarters of the height of your budding knight.
- Cut a small notch at either end to hold the string and stop it from slipping.
- Tie a length of string from the top to the bottom and tighten.
- Cut smaller, straight sticks for arrows.
- Peel off the bark to make them stand out.
- Arrows don't need arrow heads and are safer without them. They will fire dramatic distances so make sure you make plenty to replace the lost ones.

A catapult
- Find a stick with a y-shaped fork.
- Shorten the top branches of the 'y' to about 8cm/3in and the handle to a manageable size for your hands.
- About 3cm/1in down, cut a notch in the bark and tie a length of rubber (a thick rubber band will work well) to both sides of the 'y'.
- Give yourself just enough length to pull back slightly.
- Find some ammunition and fire, well away from others.
- Set up a tin can or bottle (something fairly light which will topple over when hit) and improve your aim with practice.
- Hold a competition if there are several of you and see who can hit the can from the greatest distance.

Hedgehog

THINGS I'VE DONE

PLACES I'VE BEEN

MY GREATEST ADVENTURE

_____

_____

_____

_____

_____

_____

_____

_____

_____

_____

_____

_____

THE END